New

Life of the
Christmas Party

(A separate Lyric Booklet is also available)

Project Manager: Carol Cuellar
Book Art Layout: Ken Rehm
Cover Image: ©1998 PhotoDisc, Inc.

Contents

A-CAROLING WE GO

Words and Music by
JOHNNY MARKS

house to house we bring the mes-sage of the King a-gain.}
join us if you will as we are sing-ing once a-gain.}

Chorus

Peace on ____ earth, good will to men, peace on ____ earth, good

1. 2. 3.
will to men. ____

4.
2. We will to men. ____

3. Now you may have your holly and perhaps some mistletoe,
   Maybe a fir tree and maybe snow.
   But wouldn't it be wonderful if we could have again.   (to Chorus)

4. A caroling, a caroling, a caroling we go.
   Hearts filled with music and cheeks a-glow.
   From house to house we bring the message of the King again.   (to Chorus)

ANGELS WE HAVE HEARD ON HIGH

TRADITIONAL FRENCH CAROL

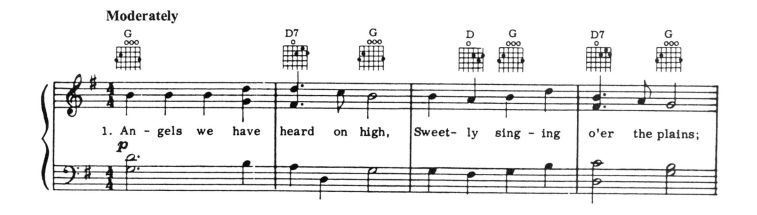

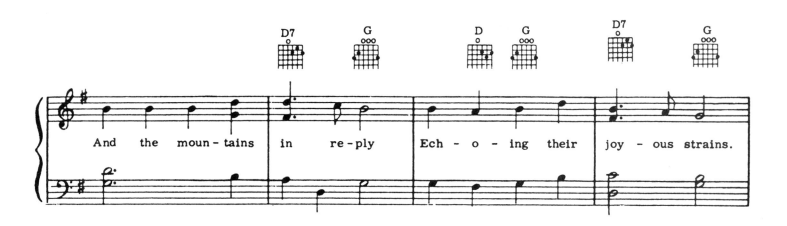

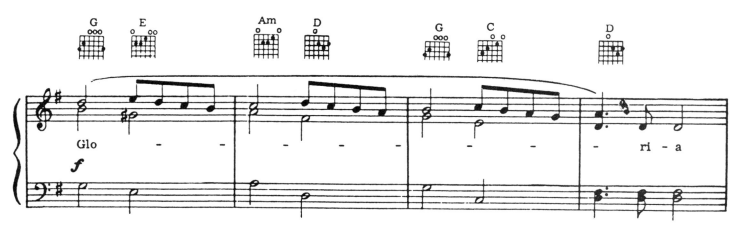

Angels We Have Heard on High - 2 - 1

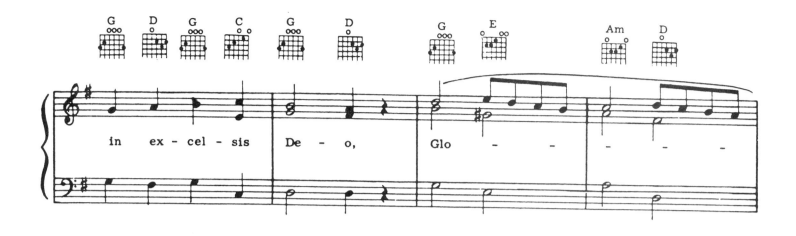

in ex - cel - sis De - o,   Glo - - - - - -

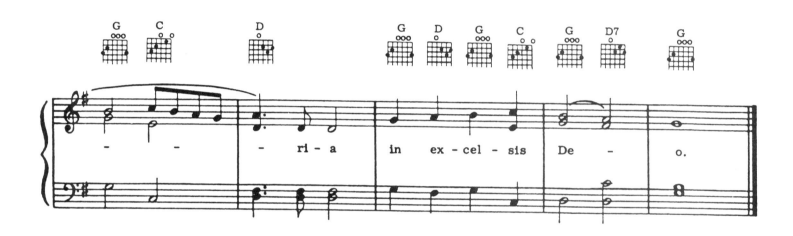

- - - ri - a   in ex - cel - sis   De - o.

2. Shepherds, why this jubilee?
   Why your joyous songs prolong?
   What the gladsome tidings be
   Which inspire your heav'nly song?
   Gloria in excelsis Deo,
   Gloria in excelsis Deo.

3. Come to Bethlehem and see
   Him whose birth the angels sing;
   Come, adore on bended knee,
   Christ, the Lord, our new-born King.
   Gloria in excelsis Deo,
   Gloria in excelsis Deo.

Angels We Have Heard on High - 2 - 2

ANGELS FROM THE REALMS OF GLORY

Words by
JAMES MONTGOMERY

Music by
HENRY SMART

Moderately

1. An - gels from the realms of glo - ry, Wing your flight o'er all the earth,

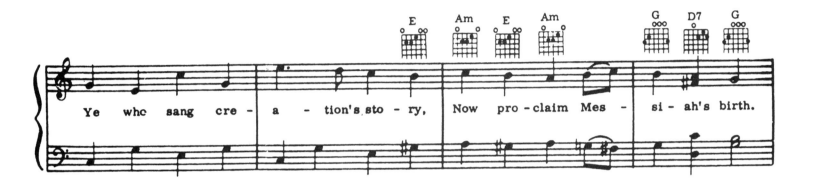

Ye who sang cre - a - tion's sto - ry, Now pro - claim Mes - si - ah's birth.

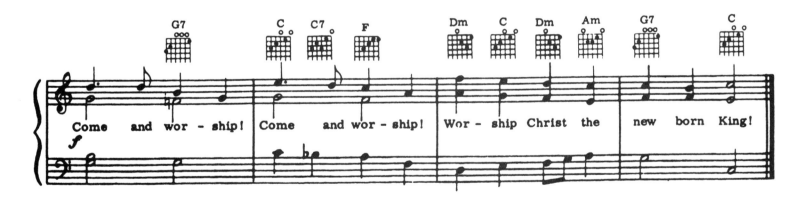

Come and wor - ship! Come and wor - ship! Wor - ship Christ the new born King!

2. Shepherds in the fields abiding,
   Watching o'er your flocks by night,
   God with man is now residing
   Yonder shines the infant Light.
   Come and worship! etc.

3. Sages, leave your contemplations
   Brighter visions beam afar,
   Seek the great Desire of nations
   Ye have seen His natal star.
   Come and worship! etc.

AULD LANG SYNE

Words by ROBERT BURNS
TRADITIONAL SCOTTISH AIR

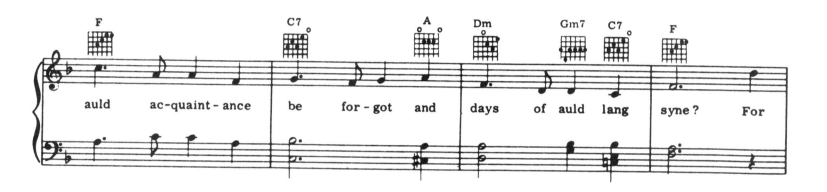

AWAY IN A MANGER

Words and Music by
J.E. SPILLMAN
and MARTIN LUTHER

Away in the Manger - 2 - 1

Away in the Manger - 2 - 2

THE BELLS OF CHRISTMAS
(Hear the Bells)

Words and Music by
MARY STUART

The Bells Of Christmas - 2 - 2

THE BOAR'S HEAD CAROL

TRADITIONAL

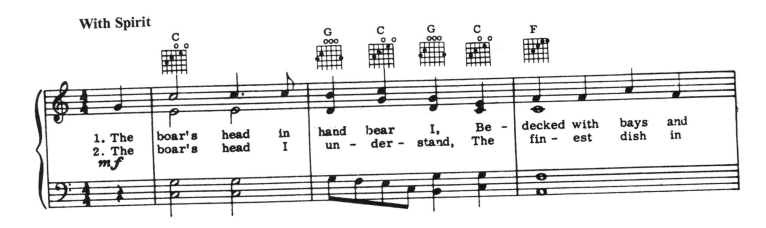

Refrain:

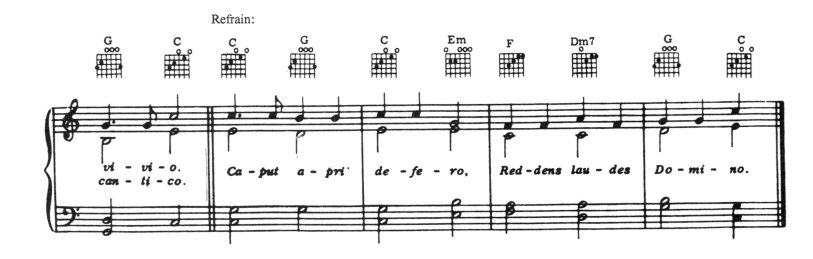

BRIGHT AND JOYFUL IS THE MORN

Words by
JAMES MONTGOMERY

WELSH HYMN

BRING A TORCH, JEANNETTE ISABELLA

TRADITIONAL FRENCH

CAROLING, CAROLING

Lyrics by
WIHLA HUTSON

Music by
ALFRED BURT

A CHILD THIS DAY IS BORN

TRADITIONAL

Verse 2:
These tidings shepherds heard
In field watching their fold,
Were by an angel unto them
That night revealed and told: *(Refrain:)*

Verse 3:
And as the angel told them,
So to them did appear;
They found the young Child, Jesus Christ,
With Mary, His Mother dear: *(Refrain:)*

THE CHIPMUNK SONG
(Christmas, Don't Be Late)

Moderate waltz ♩. = 52

By ROSS BAGDASARIAN, SR.

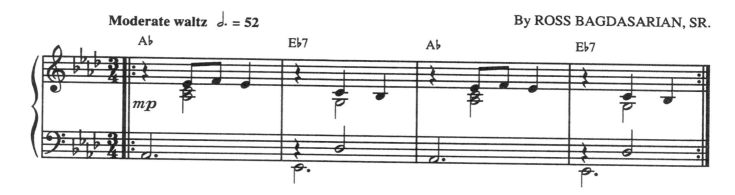

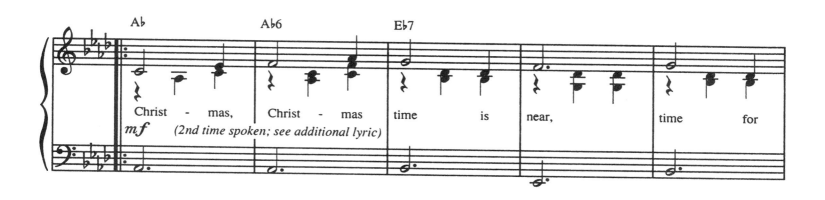

Christ - mas, Christ - mas time is near, time for

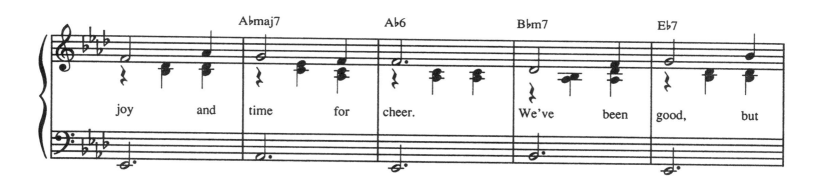

joy and time for cheer. We've been good, but

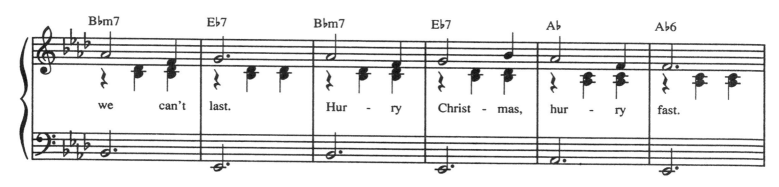

we can't last. Hur - ry Christ - mas, hur - ry fast.

The Chipmunk Song - 3 - 1

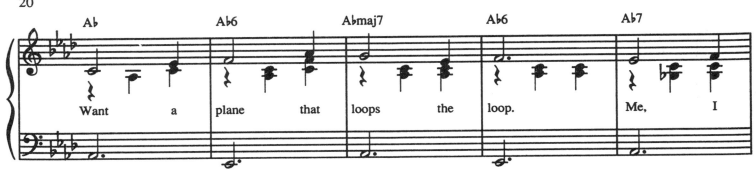

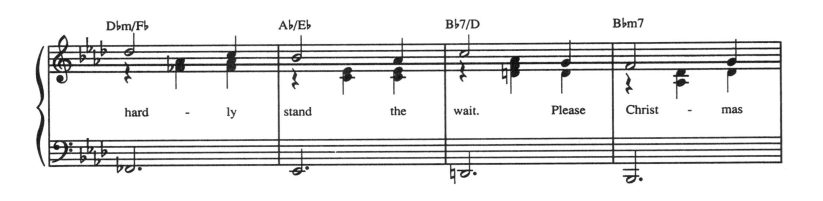

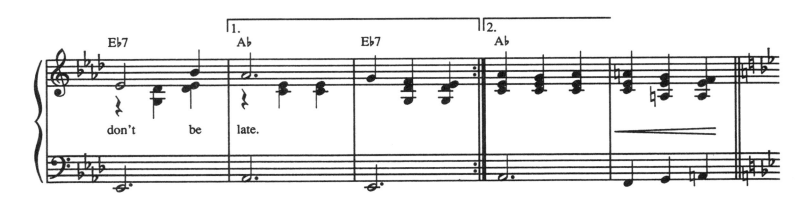

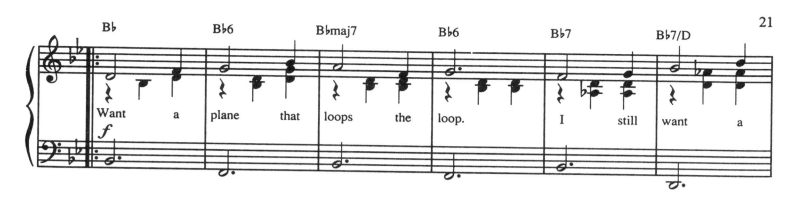

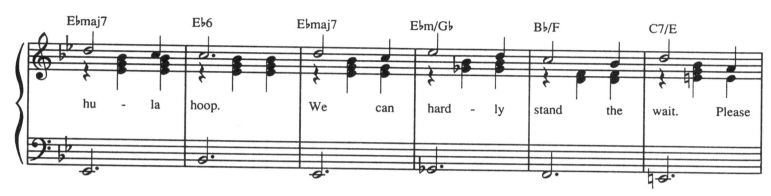

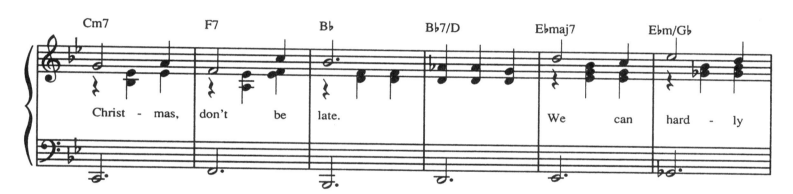

Additional lyric spoken:
Alvin: *Dave, I've been asking for that hula hoop for years.*
I would like to ask for something new,
Like roller skates, or a new stereo.
But I've just got to get that hula hoop first.
Please Dave?
I feel I've been very patient.
Dave: *Alvin, just finish the song.*
We'll talk about it later.

The Chipmunk Song - 3 - 3

CHRISTMAS AULD LANG SYNE

Words and Music by
MANN CURTIS and FRANK MILITARY

Slowly, with deep expression

Refrain

When mis - tle-toe and tin - sel glow paint a Yule-tide Val - en -

tine; Back home I go to those I know, for a CHRIST-MAS AULD LANG

SYNE. And as we gath - er 'round the tree, our voic - es all com -

bine In sweet ac - cord to thank the Lord for a CHRIST-MAS AULD LANG

Christmas Auld Lang Syne - 2 - 1

Christmas Auld Lang Syne - 2 - 2

CHRISTMAS IN THE CITY

Words and Music by
JAY LEONHART

Christmas in the City - 4 - 4

CHRISTMAS EVE

Words and Music by
MARIA CHRISTENSEN
and CURT FRASCA

Christmas Eve - 6 - 1

Verse:

1. Snow_____ fall - ing, gent - ly to_____ the ground..
2. We're stay - in' up late to - night, dec - o - rate_____ the tree._____

'Tis the night be - fore, and
Just look in - to my eyes and

in my heart___ there is_____ no doubt_____ that this is
I will tell___ you truth - ful - ly_____ that I don't

gon - na be the bright - est hol - i - day,_____
need no San - ta Claus to hear my Christ - mas list._____

31

Christmas Eve - 6 - 4

32

Christmas Eve - 6 - 5

CHRISTMAS EVE IN MY HOME TOWN

Christmas Eve in My Home Town - 3 - 1

THE CHRISTMAS WALTZ

Words by
SAMMY CAHN

Music by
JULE STYNE

The Christmas Waltz - 3 - 1

38

The Christmas Waltz - 3 - 2

The Christmas Waltz - 3 - 3

COME, ALL YE SHEPHERDS

CZECH CAROL

Gaily

1. Come, all ye shep - herds such won - ders en - thrall.

Come where the young Child is laid in a stall.

This day to us a Sav - ior is giv - en. Whom God on high hath sent down from heav - en.

Hal - le - lu - jah!

2. Come hear what wonderful tidings are fraught.
In Bethlehem see what joy they have brought.
Good will from heaven to man is given,
Peace never ending to earth descending,
Glory to God!

3. Haste then to Bethlehem, there to behold
Jesus the Babe of whom angels have told.
There to His glory tell we the story,
Glad voices raising Him over praising,
Hallelujah!

DECK THE HALL

TRADITIONAL OLD WELSH

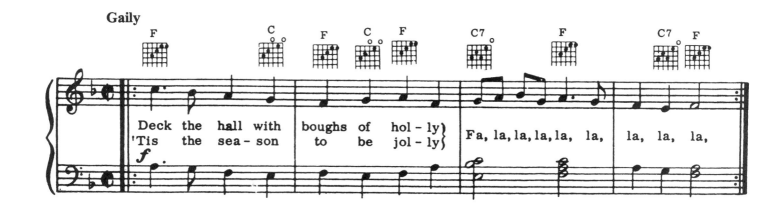

Deck the hall with boughs of hol-ly)
'Tis the sea-son to be jol-ly}
Fa, la, la, la, la, la, la, la, la,

Don we now our gay ap-par-el, Fa, la, la, la, la, la, la, la, la,

Troll the an-cient Yule-tide car-ol, Fa, la, la, la, la, la, la, la, la.

DON'T SAVE IT ALL FOR CHRISTMAS DAY

Words and Music by
PETER ZIZZO, RIC WAKE
and CELINE DION

48

Verse 2:
How could you wait another minute,
A hug is warmer when you're in it.
And, baby, that's a fact.
And sayin' I love you's always better,
Seasons, reasons, they don't matter.
So don't hold back.
How many people in this world
So needful in this world?
How many people are praying for love?
(To Chorus:)

THE FIRST NOEL

TRADITIONAL ENGLISH CAROL

EVERYONE'S A CHILD AT CHRISTMAS

Words and Music by
JOHNNY MARKS

Everyone's a Child at Christmas - 2 - 2

GATHER AROUND THE CHRISTMAS TREE

By
JOHN HOPKINS

THE MAGIC OF CHRISTMAS DAY
(God Bless Everyone)

Words and Music by
DEE SNIDER

54

56

The Magic of Christmas Day - 5 - 5

THE GINGERBREAD HOUSE

Words and Music by
ROGER LaVOIE

GOD REST YE MERRY, GENTLEMEN

TRADITIONAL ENGLISH CAROL

ti - dings of com - fort and joy, com-fort and joy, o ——— ti - dings of com - fort and joy.

3. In Bethlehem, in Jewry
This blessed Babe was born,
And laid within a manger
Upon this holy morn,
The which his Mother Mary
Did nothing take in scorn.
    O tidings, etc.

4. "Fear not then," said the Angel,
"Let nothing you affright,
This day is born a Saviour
Of a pure Virgin bright,
To free all those who trust in Him
From Satan's power and might."
    O tidings, etc.

5. The shepherds at those tidings
Rejoiced much in mind,
And left their flocks a-feeding,
In tempest, storm, and wind:
And went to Bethlehem straightway,
The Song of God to find.
    O tidings, etc.

6. And when they came to Bethlehem
Where our dear Saviour lay,
They found Him in a manger,
Where oxen feed on hay;
His Mother Mary kneeling down,
Unto the Lord did pray.
    O tidings, etc.

7. Now to the Lord sing praises,
All you within this place,
And with true love and brotherhood
Each other now embrace;
This holy tide of Christmas
All other doth deface.
    O tidings, etc.

GOOD CHRISTIAN MEN, REJOICE

Words by
JOHN MASON NEALE

OLD GERMAN CAROL

2. Good Christian men, rejoice
With heart and soul and voice,
Now ye hear of endless bliss;
Joy! Joy! Jesus Christ was born for this.
He hath ope'd the heav'nly door,
And man is blessed evermore;
Christ was born for this.
Christ was born for this.

3. Good Christian men, rejoice
With heart and soul and voice,
Now ye need not fear the grave:
Peace! Peace! Jesus Christ was born to save.
Calls you one and calls you all,
To gain His everlasting hall;
Christ was born to save.
Christ was born to save.

GOOD KING WENCESLAS

TRADITIONAL ENGLISH CAROL

2. "Hither, page, and stand by me,
If thou know'st it telling,
Yonder peasant, who is he?
Where and what his dwelling?"
"Sire, he lives a good league hence,
Underneath the mountain,
Right against the forest fence,
By St. Agnes' fountain."

3. "Bring me flesh, and bring me wine,
Bring me pine logs hither;
Thou and I will see him dine,
When we bear them thither."
Page and monarch, forth they went,
Forth they went together;
Through the rude wind's wild lament,
And the bitter weather.

4. "Sire, the night is darker now,
And the wind blows stronger;
Fails my heart, I know not how;
I can go no longer."
"Mark my footsteps my good page,
Tread thou in them boldly:
Thou shalt find the winter's rage
Freeze thy blood less coldly."

5. In his master's steps he trod,
Where the snow lay dinted;
Heat was in the very sod
Which the Saint had printed.
Therefore, Christian men, be sure,
Wealth or rank possessing,
Ye who now will bless the poor,
Shall yourselves find blessing.

GRANDMA GOT RUN OVER
BY A REINDEER!

Words and Music by
RANDY BROOKS

Grandma Got Run Over by a Reindeer! - 5 - 1

66

Grandma Got Run Over by a Reindeer! - 5 - 3

Verse 2:
Now we're all so proud of Grandpa,
He's been taking this so well.
See him in there watching football,
Drinking beer and playing cards with Cousin Mel.
It's not Christmas without Grandma.
All the family's dressed in black,
And we just can't help but wonder:
Should we open up her gifts or send them back?

(To Chorus:)

Verse 3:
Now the goose is on the table,
And the pudding made of fig,
And the blue and silver candles,
That would just have matched the hair in Grandma's wig.
I've warned all my friends and neighbors,
Better watch out for yourselves.
They should never give a license
To a man who drives a sleigh and plays with elves.

(To Chorus:)

Grandma Got Run Over by a Reindeer! - 5 - 5

HARK! THE BELLS ARE RINGING

TRADITIONAL

A GREAT AND MIGHTY WONDER

GERMAN

A Great and Mighty Wonder - 2 - 1

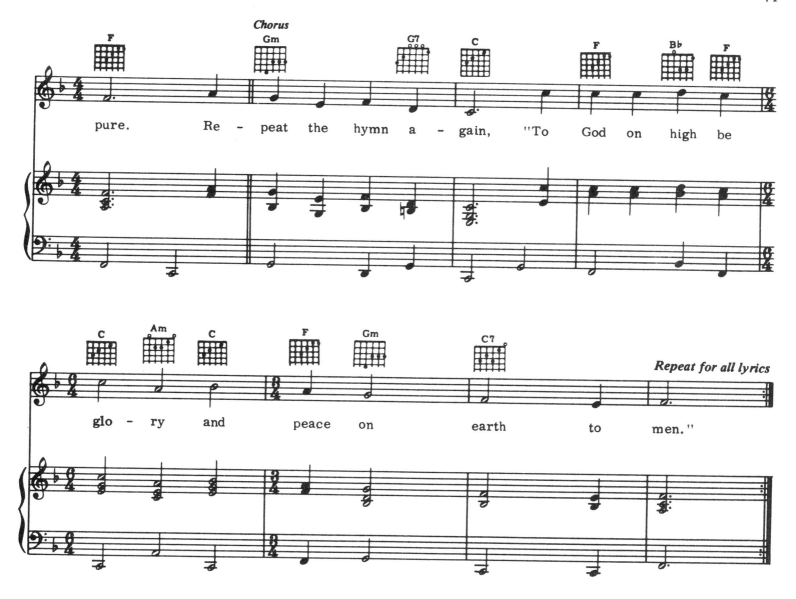

Chorus

pure. Re - peat the hymn a - gain, "To God on high be

glo - ry and peace on earth to men."

Repeat for all lyrics

2. The Word becomes incarnate
    And yet remains on high!
    And cherubim sing anthems
    To shepherds from the sky.

3. While thus they sing your Monarch,
    Those bright angelic bands
    Rejoice, ye vales and mountains,
    Ye oceans, clap your hands.

4. Since all He comes to ransom,
    By all be He adorned,
    The infant born in Bethl'em,
    The Saviour and the Lord.

5. And idol forms shall perish,
    And error shall decay,
    And Christ shall wield His sceptre,
    Our Lord and God for aye.

A Great and Mighty Wonder - 2 - 2

HARK! THE HERALD ANGELS SING

Words by
CHARLES WESLEY

Music by
FELIX MENDELSSOHN

1. Hark! the her - ald an - gels sing,___ "Glo - ry to the new - born king!
3. Hail the heav'n born Prince of Peace!___ Hail the Sun of right - eous - ness!

Peace on earth and mer - cy mild;___ God and sin - ners re - con - ciled."
Light and life to all He brings,___ Ris'n with heal - ing in His wings.

Hark! The Herald Angels Sing - 3 - 1

Hark! the Herald Angels Sing - 3 - 2

HERE COMES SANTA CLAUS
(Right Down Santa Claus Lane)

Words and Music by
GENE AUTRY and
OAKLEY HALDEMAN

HAVE YOURSELF A MERRY LITTLE CHRISTMAS
(Have Yourself a Blessed Little Christmas)

Sacred Lyrics by
HUGH MARTIN and JOHN FRICKE

Words and Music by
HUGH MARTIN and RALPH BLANE

Have yourself a merry little Christmas, let your heart be light,
From now on, our troubles will be out of sight.
Have yourself a merry little Christmas, make the Yule-tide gay,
From now on, our troubles will be miles away.

Have Yourself a Merry Little Christmas - 2 - 1

Have Yourself a Merry Little Christmas - 2 - 2

HERE WE COME A-WASSAILING

OLD ENGLISH

Here We Come A-Wassailing - 2 - 1

2. We are not daily beggars
   That beg from door to door;
   But we are neighbors' children
   Whom you have seen before.

   Chorus

3. We have got a little purse,
   Of stretching leather skin;
   We want a little of your money
   To line it well within.

   Chorus

4. Bring us out a table,
   And spread it with a cloth;
   Bring us out a mouldy cheese,
   And some of your Christmas loaf.

   Chorus

5. God bless the master of this house,
   Likewise the mistress too;
   And all the little children
   That round the table go.

   Chorus

Here We Come A-Wassailing - 2 - 2

HOLIDAY TIME IS NEAR

Words and Music by
LEONARD C. CHRISTMAN

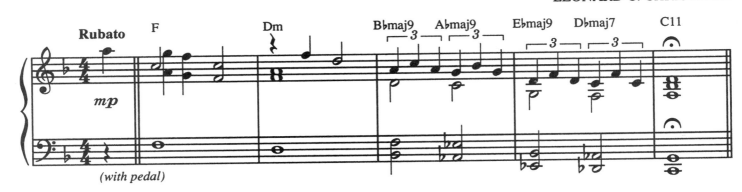

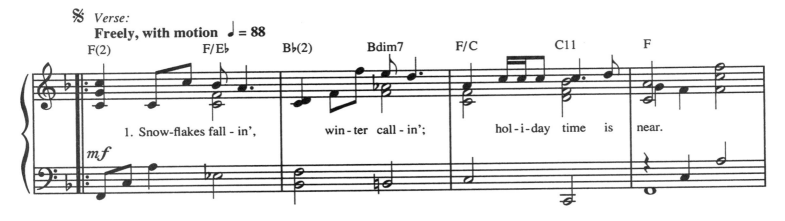

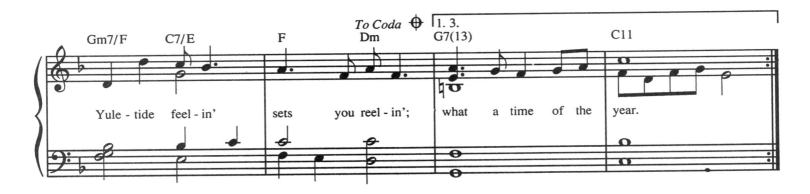

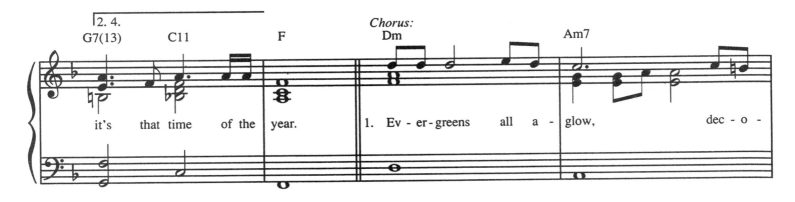

Holiday Time Is Near - 3 - 1

Holiday Time Is Near - 3 - 2

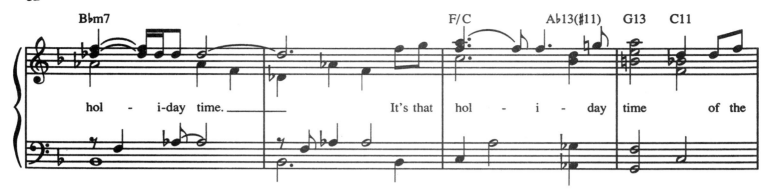

hol - i-day time. _____ It's that hol - i - day time of the

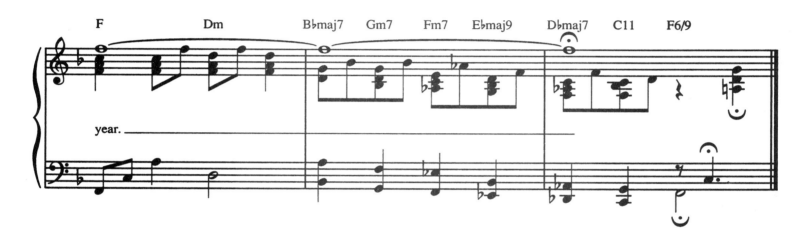

year. _____

Verse 2:
Window shoppin', toy store hoppin'; holiday time is near.
Popcorn stringin', carol singin'; it's that time of the year.
(To Chorus 1:)

Verse 3:
Candy makin', cookie bakin'; holiday time is near.
Chestnut roastin', family toastin', what a time of the year.

Verse 4:
Children dreamin', faces beamin'; holiday time is near.
Present wrappin' while they're nappin'; it's that time of the year.

Chorus 2:
Sleigh rides in the snow, holly wreaths and mistletoe,
Santa's on his way; soon it will be Christmas Day.
And I love the sound of...

Verse 5:
People greetin' when they're meetin', sharin' their Christmas cheer.
Congregatin', celebratin'; ringin' in the New Year.
(To Coda)

THE HOLLY AND THE IVY

TRADITIONAL ENGLISH

2. The holly bears a blossom,
As white as lily flow'r,
And Mary bore sweet Jesus Christ,
To be our sweet Saviour.

Refrain:

3. The Holly bears a berry,
As red as any blood,
And Mary bore sweet Jesus Christ,
To do poor sinners good.

Refrain:

A HOLLY JOLLY CHRISTMAS

Words and Music by
JOHNNY MARKS

HOLY NIGHT, PEACEFUL NIGHT

SIR JOSEPH BARNBY

Gently, with feeling

Holy Night, Peaceful Night - 2 - 1

Rests in heav'n - ly peace, _____ Rests in heav'n - ly peace. _____
Je - sus Christ _____ is here! _____ Je - sus Christ _____ is here!" _____

rit.

Holy Night, Peaceful Night - 2 - 2

(There's No Place Like)

HOME FOR THE HOLIDAYS

Words by
AL STILLMAN

Music by
ROBERT ALLEN

Home for the Holidays - 2 - 1

Home for the Holidays - 2 - 2

HURRAY FOR CHRISTMAS

Words and Music by
DON SEBESKY

92

Hurray for Christmas - 4 - 4

I HEARD THE BELLS ON CHRISTMAS DAY

Words by
HENRY WADSWORTH LONGFELLOW
(Adapted by JOHN MARKS)

Music by
JOHN MARKS

I WANT AN OLD-FASHIONED CHRISTMAS

Words by
FLORENCE TARR

Music by
FAY FOSTER

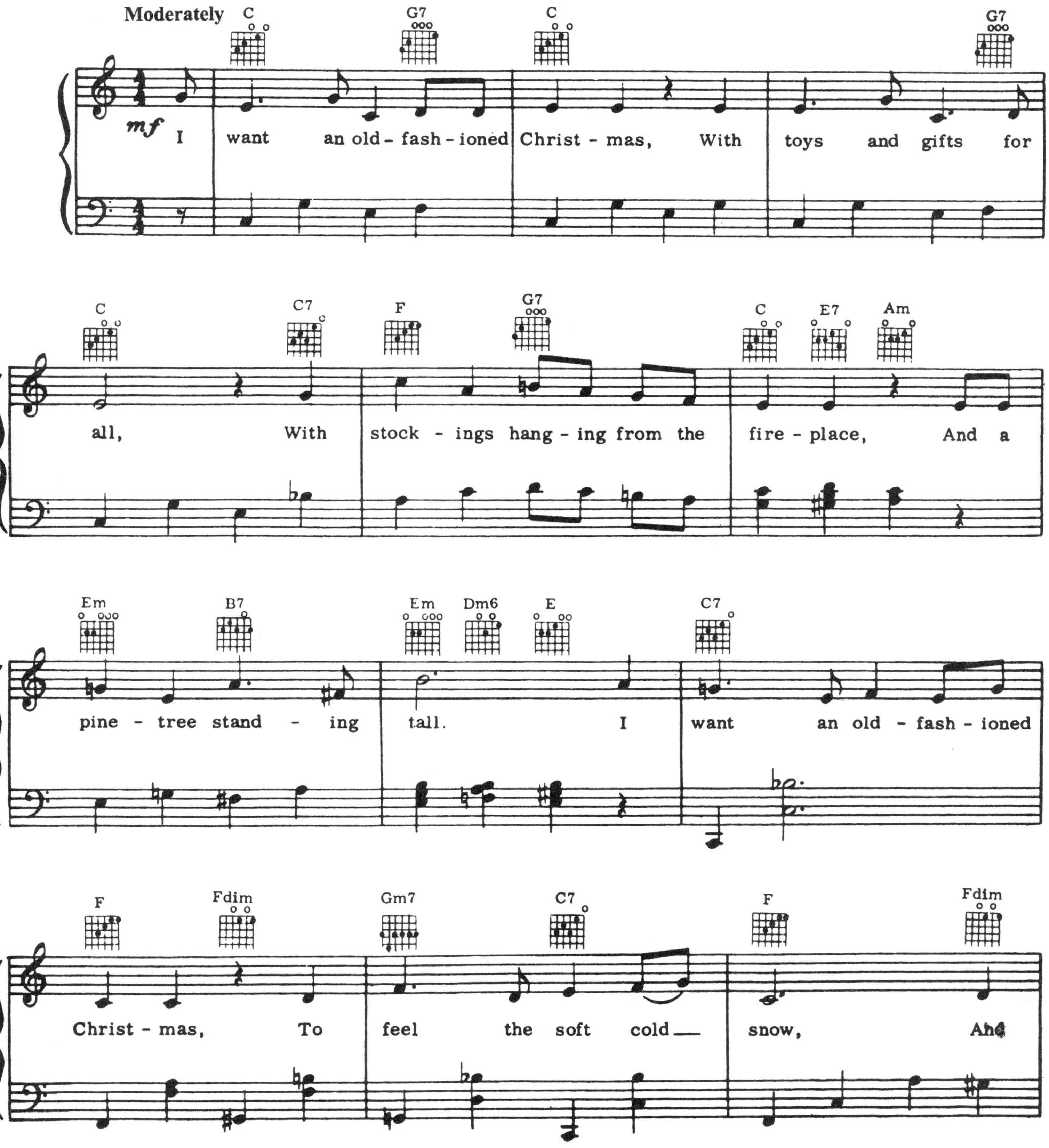

Moderately

I want an old-fash-ioned Christ-mas, With toys and gifts for

all, With stock-ings hang-ing from the fire-place, And a

pine-tree stand-ing tall. I want an old-fash-ioned

Christ-mas, To feel the soft cold snow, Ah

I Want an Old-Fashioned Christmas - 3 - 1

96

I Want an Old-Fashioned Christmas - 3 - 2

I Want an Old-Fashioned Christmas - 3 - 3

I'LL BE HOME FOR CHRISTMAS

Lyric by
KIM GANNON

Music by
WALTER KENT

99

I'll Be Home for Christmas - 2 - 2

In A Christmas Mood

Lyric by
JUDY SPENCER

Music by
EARL ROSE

*Melody sung one octave lower

In a Christmas Mood - 3 - 1

IT MUST HAVE BEEN THE MISTLETOE

Words and Music by
JUSTIN WILDE and DOUG KONECKY

It must have been the mis-tle-toe, __ the la-zy fire, __ the fall-ing snow, __ the mag-ic in __ the frost-y air; __ that feel-ing ev-'ry-where. It must have been __ the pret-ty lights __ that glis-tened __ in the si-lent night, __ or

It Must Have Been the Mistletoe - 5 - 1

104

IT CAME UPON THE MIDNIGHT CLEAR

Words by
EDMUND H. SEARS

Music by
RICHARD S. WILLIS

3. And ye beneath life's crushing load,
Whose forms are bending low,
Who toil along the climbing way
With painful steps and slow,
Look now! for glad and golden hours
Come swiftly on the wing.
O rest beside the weary road
And hear the angels sing.

4. For lo, the days are hast'ning on,
By prophet bards foretold,
When with the ever circling years
Comes round the age of gold,
When peace shall over all the earth
Its ancient splendor fling,
And the whole world give back the song
Which now the angels sing.

JINGLE BELLS

Words and Music by
JAMES PIERPONT

Jingle Bells - 2 - 1

Chorus:

JINGLE, JINGLE, JINGLE

Words and Music by
JOHNNY MARKS

Moderately, gaily

Jin - gle, jin - gle, jin - gle, you will hear his sleigh bells ring,

Jol - ly old Kris Krin - gle, is the King of jin - gl - ing.

Jin - gle, jin - gle, rein - deer, through the frost - y air they'll go,

They are not just plain deer, they're the fast - est deer I know. (Ho! Ho!) You

Jingle, Jingle, Jingle - 2 - 1

JOLLY OLD SAINT NICHOLAS

TRADITIONAL

Jolly Old Saint Nicholas - 2 - 1

Jolly Old Saint Nicholas - 2 - 2

IT'S THE MOST WONDERFUL
TIME OF THE YEAR

By EDDIE POLA
and GEORGE WYLE

117

It's the Most Wonderful Time of the Year - 3 - 2

It's the Most Wonderful Time of the Year - 3 - 3

LET IT SNOW! LET IT SNOW! LET IT SNOW!

Lyric by
SAMMY CAHN

Music by
JULE STYNE

JOYOUS CHRISTMAS

Words and Music by
JOHNNY MARKS

121

JOY TO THE WORLD

Words by
ISAAC WATTS

Music by
GEORGE F. HANDEL

room, _____ And heav'n and na - ture____ sing, And ___
plains_____ Re - peat the sound - ing____ joy, Re -
ness, _____ And won - ders of His____ love, And___

heav'n and na - ture____ sing, And___ heav'n, ____ And
peat the sound - ing____ joy, Re - peat,____ re -
won - ders of His____ love, And___ won - ders,

heav'n _____ and na - ture sing.
peat _____ the sound - ing joy.
won - ders of His love.

Joy to the World - 2 - 2

THE LITTLE DRUMMER BOY

Words and Music by
KATHERINE DAVIS, HENRY ONORATI
and HARRY SIMEONE

The Little Drummer Boy - 4 - 1

126

The Little Drummer Boy - 4 - 3

The Little Drummer Boy - 4 - 4

LITTLE SAINT NICK

Words and Music by
BRIAN WILSON

Little Saint Nick - 4 - 1

129

Little Saint Nick - 4 - 2

131

Little Saint Nick - 4 - 4

MERRY CHRISTMAS

Lyrics by
JANICE TORRE

Music by
FRED SPIELMAN

Merry Christmas - 2 - 1

133

Merry Christmas - 2 - 2

MERRY CHRISTMAS, DARLING

Lyric by
FRANK POOLER

Music by
RICHARD CARPENTER

Greet-ing cards have all been sent, the Christ-mas rush is through,

but I still have one wish to make, a spe-cial one for you:

Mer-ry Christ-mas dar-ling. We're a-part that's true, but

Merry Christmas, Darling - 3 - 1

Merry Christmas, Darling - 3 - 3

NOEL! NOEL!

TRADITIONAL

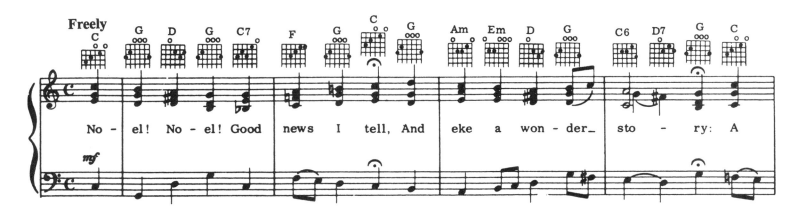

No - el! No - el! Good news I tell, And eke a won - der sto - ry: A

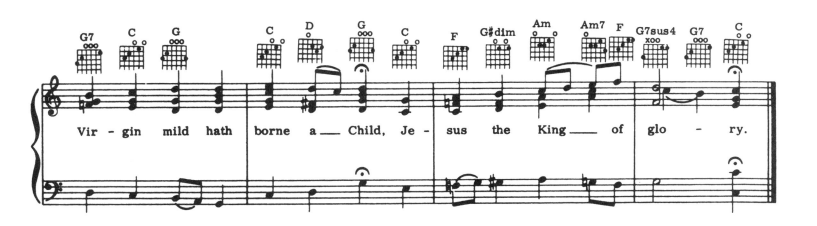

Vir - gin mild hath borne a Child, Je - sus the King of glo - ry.

A MERRY, MERRY CHRISTMAS TO YOU
(Joyeux Noel, Buon Natale, Feliz Navidad)

Words and Music by
JOHNNY MARKS

139

*Use any language desired. (**) Can repeat full chorus then 4 bar vamp shouting languages, then Coda

A Merry, Merry Christmas to You - 2 - 2

THE MOST WONDERFUL DAY
OF THE YEAR

Words and Music by
JOHNNY MARKS

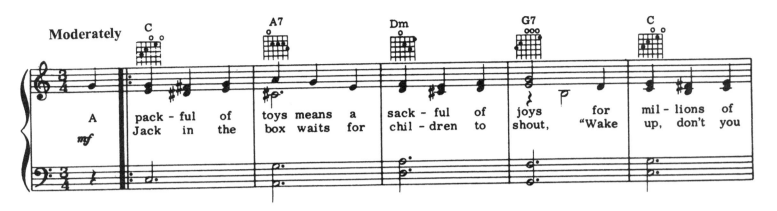

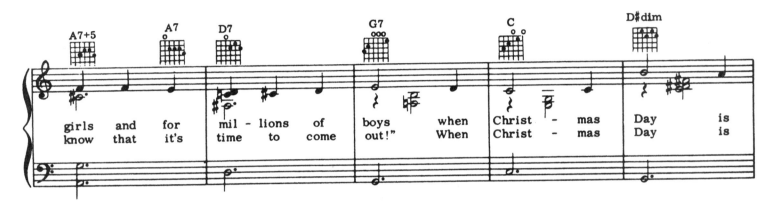

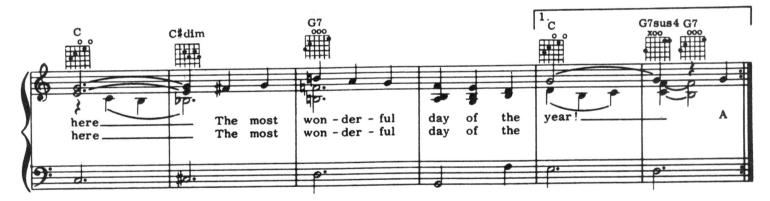

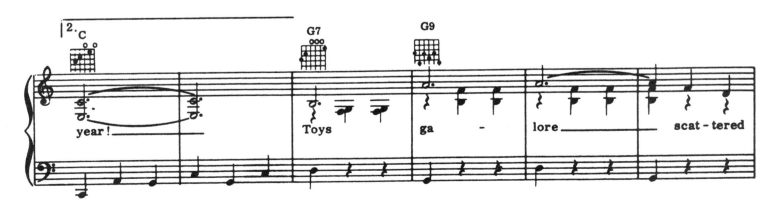

The Most Wonderful Day of the Year - 2 - 1

The Most Wonderful Day of the Year - 2 - 2

O CHRISTMAS TREE
(O Tannenbaum)

OLD GERMAN CAROL

O COME, ALL YE FAITHFUL
(Adeste Fideles)

Music by JOHN READING

With great joy

1. O come all ye faith - ful, Joy - ful and tri - um - phant, O

mf

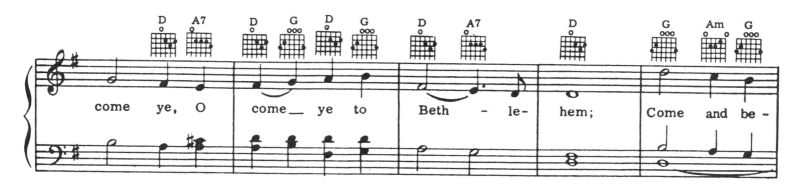

come ye, O come__ ye to Beth - le - hem; Come and be -

hold Him, Born the King of an - gels; O come let us a - dore Him, O

come let us a - dore Him, O come let us a - dore Him,— Christ__ the Lord.

2. Sing, choirs of angels,
   Sing in exultation,
   Sing, all ye citizens of heaven above:
   Glory to God
   In the highest glory!
   O come, let us adore Him, etc.

3. Yea, Lord, we greet Thee,
   Born this happy morning,
   Jesus, to Thee be glory giv'n,
   Word of the Father,
   Now in flesh appearing.
   O come, let us adore Him, etc.

O HOLY NIGHT
(Cantique de Noel)

Words by
JOHN S. DWIGHT

Music by
ADOLPHE CHARLES ADAM

O Holy Night - 4 - 1

3. Truly He taught us to love one another;
His law is love and His gospel is peace;
Chains shall He break, for the slave is our brother,
And in His name, all oppression shall cease.
With hymns of joy in grateful chorus raising,
Let every heart adore His Holy Name!
Christ is the Lord!
With saint and seraph praising,
His power and glory evermore proclaim!
His power and glory evermore proclaim!

147

O Holy Night - 4 - 4

O LITTLE TOWN OF BETHLEHEM

Words by
PHILLIS BROOKS

Music by
LEWIS H. REDNER

O Little Town of Bethlehem - 2 - 2

(There's Nothing Like)

AN OLD FASHIONED CHRISTMAS

Words and Music by
JOHNNY MARKS

An Old Fashioned Christmas - 2 - 2

THE OLD MAN'S BACK IN TOWN

Words and Music by
LARRY B. BASTIAN, RANDY TAYLOR
and GARTH BROOKS

Bright country swing ♩ = 160

Yeah, the Old Man's back in town.___ He's
spread-in' cheer a - round.___ He's come___ a long,_ long way___ with his rein-
-deer and_ his sleigh. Hey, he's bring-in' lots of toys.___ for all_

The Old Man's Back in Town - 3 - 1

E
B
— good girls and boys. — So spread — the news — a-round. — Hey, the
To Coda
E6
Verse:
E
Old Man's back in town. — 1. He's been wait-in' all — year long —
mf
A
B
— just to bring — his gifts — to you. — And all the elves, —
E
B
E
Mis-sis Claus — have been wait-in' all — year too. — Now, they're hook-in' up — his rein -
A
F#
- deer, and they're load-in' down — his sleigh. So take my ad - vice, — you best —

154

Verse 2:
Now, the mistletoe is hung,
And the tree is all aglow.
Carolers have sung
Every Christmas song they know.
And the kids are all in bed
Now with Santa on their mind.
So the scene is set, and you can bet
He'll show up any time.
(To Chorus:)

The Old Man's Back in Town - 3 - 3

ON CHRISTMAS NIGHT ALL CHRISTIANS SING

TRADITIONAL

2. Then why should men on earth be so sad,
   Since our Redeemer made us glad,
   Then why should men on earth be so sad,
   Since our Redeemer made us glad;
   When from our sin He set us free,
   All for to gain our liberty.

3. When sin departs before His grace,
   Then life and health come in its place,
   When sin departs before His grace,
   Then life and health come in its place.
   Angels and men with joy may sing,
   All for to see the new-born King.

THE ONLY THING I WANT FOR CHRISTMAS

By
VICK KNIGHT, JOHNNY LANGE
and LEW PORTER

The Only Thing I Want for Christmas - 3 - 1

158

RUDOLPH, THE RED-NOSED REINDEER

Words and Music by
JOHNNY MARKS

160

Rudolph, the Red-Nosed Reindeer - 3 - 2

Rudolph, the Red-Nosed Reindeer - 3 - 3

ROCKIN' AROUND THE CHRISTMAS TREE

Words and Music by
JOHNNY MARKS

Rockin' Around the Christmas Tree - 2 - 1

SANTA CLAUS IS COMIN' TO TOWN

Words by
HAVEN GILLESPIE

Music by
J. FRED COOTS

Santa Claus Is Comin' to Town - 2 - 2

THE SECRET OF CHRISTMAS

Words by
SAMMY CAHN

Music by
JAMES VAN HEUSEN

The Secret of Christmas - 2 - 1

SILENT NIGHT

Words by
JOSEPH MOHR

Music by
FRANZ GRUBER

From the Videocraft T.V. Musical Spectacular "RUDOLPH THE RED-NOSED REINDEER"

SILVER AND GOLD

Words and Music by
JOHNNY MARKS

Slowly and expressively

SLEIGH RIDE

Words by
MITCHELL PARISH

Music by
LEROY ANDERSON

Just hear those sleigh bells jin - gle - ing, ring - ting - tin - gle - ing, too, ___

___ Come on, it's love - ly weath - er for a Sleigh Ride to - geth - er with you, ___

___ Out - side the snow is fall - ing and friends are call - ing "Yoo hoo," ___

Sleigh Ride - 3 - 1

THE STAR OF CHRISTMAS MORNING

TRADITIONAL ENGLISH CAROL

2. Oh! ever thought be of His name
On Christmas in the morning,
Who bore for us both grief and shame
Affliction's sharpest scorning.
And may we die when death shall come,
On Christmas in the morning,
And see in heav'n our glorious home,
That star of Christmas morning.

THERE IS NO CHRISTMAS
LIKE A HOME CHRISTMAS

Words by
CARL SIGMAN

Music by
MICKEY J. ADDY

177

There Is No Christmas Like a Home Christmas - 2 - 2

THIRTY-TWO FEET AND EIGHT LITTLE TAILS
(Dasher, Dancer, Prancer, Vixen, Comet, Cupid, Donner, Blitzen)

Words and Music by
JOHN REDMOND, JAMES CAVANAUGH
and FRANK WELDON

Thirty-Two Feet and Eight Little Tails - 2 - 1

Thirty-Two Feet and Eight Little Tails - 2 - 2

THE TWELVE DAYS OF CHRISTMAS

TRADITIONAL

The Twelve Days of Christmas - 3 - 2

182

The Twelve Days of Christmas - 3 - 3

THESE ARE THE SPECIAL TIMES

Words and Music by
DIANE WARREN

These Are the Special Times - 5 - 1

184

These Are the Special Times - 5 - 3

These Are the Special Times - 5 - 5

TOYLAND

Words by
GLEN MacDONOUGH

Music by
VICTOR HERBERT

UP ON THE HOUSE-TOP

Words and Music by
BENJAMIN RUSSELL HANBY

UKRAINIAN CAROL

TRADITIONAL

Ukranian Carol - 2 - 1

From the Videocraft T.V. Musical Spectacular "RUDOLPH THE RED-NOSED REINDEER"

WE ARE SANTA'S ELVES

Words and Music by
JOHNNY MARKS

Ho! Ho! Ho! Ho! Ho! Ho! We are San - ta's elves!

We are San - ta's elves, fil - ling San - ta's shelves
We work hard all day, but our work is play.
San - ta knows who's good; do the things you should!

We Are Santa's Elves - 2 - 1

with a toy for each girl and boy. Oh, we are San - ta's elves!
Dolls we try out, see if they cry out, we are San - ta's elves!
And we bet you, he won't for-get you, we are San - ta's elves!

We've a spe - cial job each year, we don't like to brag.

Christ-mas Eve we al-ways fill San - ta's bag! _____

Ho! Ho! Ho! Ho! Ho! Ho! We are San - ta's elves! Ho! Ho!

WE THREE KINGS OF ORIENT ARE

Words and Music by
Rev. JOHN HENRY HOPKINS

WHAT CHILD IS THIS?

By WILLIAM C. DIX

Based on GREENSLEEVES,
an Old English Air

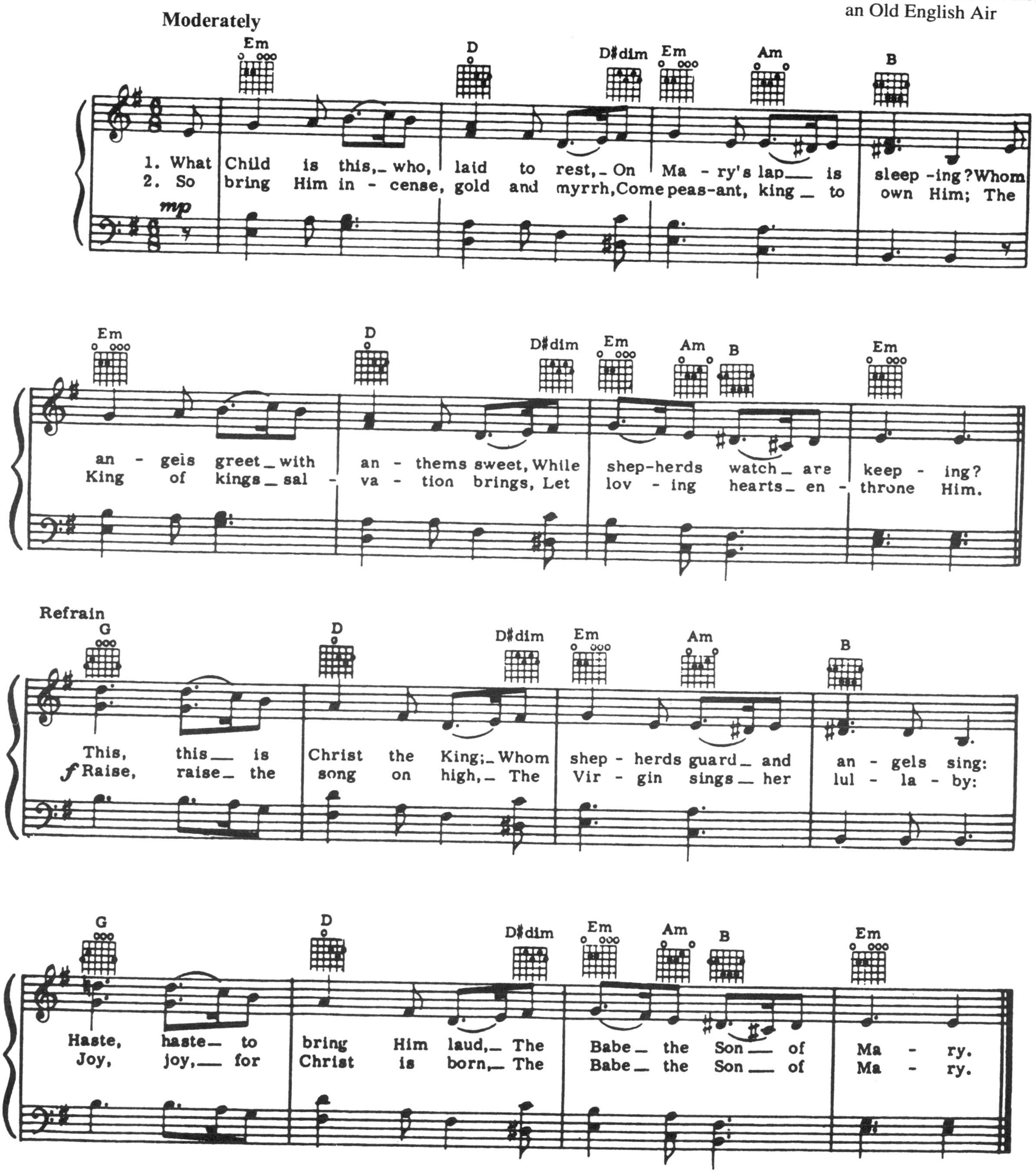

Moderately
Em
D
D#dim
Em
Am
B
mp
1. What Child is this, who, laid to rest, On Ma - ry's lap is sleep - ing? Whom
2. So bring Him in - cense, gold and myrrh, Come peas - ant, king to own Him; The
Em
D
D#dim
Em
Am
B
Em
an - gels greet with an - thems sweet, While shep - herds watch are keep - ing?
King of kings sal - va - tion brings, Let lov - ing hearts en - throne Him.
Refrain
G
D
D#dim
Em
Am
B
This, this is Christ the King; Whom shep - herds guard and an - gels sing:
f Raise, raise the song on high, The Vir - gin sings her lul - la - by:
G
D
D#dim
Em
Am
B
Em
Haste, haste to bring Him laud, The Babe the Son of Ma - ry.
Joy, joy, for Christ is born, The Babe the Son of Ma - ry.

WE WISH YOU A MERRY CHRISTMAS

TRADITIONAL ENGLISH FOLK SONG

We Wish You a Merry Christmas - 2 - 2

WHEN SANTA CLAUS GETS YOUR LETTER

Words and Music by
JOHNNY MARKS

When Santa Claus Gets Your Letter - 2 - 1

When Santa Claus Gets Your Letter - 2 - 2

WINTER WONDERLAND

Words by
DICK SMITH

Music by
FELIX BERNARD

201

Winter Wonderland - 2 - 2

THE WONDERFUL WORLD OF CHRISTMAS

Words by
CHARLES TOBIAS

Music by
AL FRISCH

The Wonderful World of Christmas - 2 - 1

203

The Wonderful World of Christmas - 2 - 2

WHILE SHEPHERDS WATCHED THEIR FLOCKS BY NIGHT

Words by
REV. NAHUM TATE and NICHOLAS BRODY

Music by
GEORGE FREDERICK HANDEL

1. While shep - herds watched their flocks by night, all seat - ed on the ground, the an - gel of the Lord came down, and glo - ry shone a - round, and glo - ry shone a - round.

2. "Fear not!" said he; for might - y dread had seized their trou - bled mind. "Glad tid - ings of great joy I bring, to you and all man - kind, to you and all man - kind."

3. "To you, in David's town, this day
Is born of David's line,
The Saviour Who is Christ the Lord;
And this shall be the sign;
And this shall be the sign."

4. "The Heav'nly Babe you there shall find
To human view displayed,
All meanly wrapped in swathingbands,
And in a manger laid,
And in a manger laid."

5. "All glory be to God on high
And to the earth be peace:
Goodwill hence forth from heav'n to men,
Begin and never cease:
Begin and never cease."